INTERMEDIATE 1

2008

[BLANK PAGE]

X115/101

NATIONAL QUALIFICATIONS 2008

THURSDAY, 15 MAY
1.00 PM – 1.45 PM

ENGLISH
INTERMEDIATE 1
Close Reading

Answer all questions.

30 marks are allocated to this paper.

Read the passage carefully and then answer **all** the questions, **using your own words where asked to do so**.

The questions will ask you to show that:

you understand **what** the writer has said (main ideas and supporting details) (**Understanding–U**);

you can identify **how** the writer has said it (techniques of structure and style) (**Analysis–A**);

you can comment on **how well** the writer has achieved his purpose (using appropriate evidence) (**Evaluation–E**).

A code letter (U, A, E) is used alongside each question to identify its purpose for you.

In this passage, the writer tells us about a famous Scottish mystery.

THE ISLAND OF LOST SOULS

Seven lumps of rock 30 miles off the west coast of Lewis, the outermost of the Outer Hebrides, the Flannan Islands have a good claim to be the most deserted place in Britain. The only inhabitants are thousands of puffins, some nesting fulmars, the "little people" of Gaelic folklore and the ghosts. But I have longed to visit the Flannans ever since, when I was a little boy, my father would scare us into delighted terror with the story of the Flannan lighthouse, one of the strangest unsolved mysteries in Scottish history.

The story goes like this: for centuries the Seven Hunters, as the local people called the islands, had preyed on shipping. Innumerable vessels had perished on the rocks, including remnants of the Spanish Armada. So the Victorians, with the spirit typical of the age, decided to build a lighthouse here, on the edge of the world.

A year after the lighthouse was lit, a steamer from Oban was sent out to relieve the three lighthouse keepers, who had been on the island, alone, for three months. As the ship approached in the morning gloom, her master could see no lights on the island. Captain Harvie sent two men scrambling up the cliff. The gate to the lighthouse enclosure was bolted, but the door of the lighthouse itself was open. Food lay uneaten on the table. Two sets of boots and oilskins had gone, but the third was still in the rack. The entries in the lighthouse log ended abruptly a week earlier, and the clocks had wound down. A chair lay on its back, but otherwise there was no sign of violence. The lamp was filled with paraffin, and the beds were neatly made. Of the three lighthouse keepers there was not a sign. The mystery remains unsolved, though many have put forward theories. For more than 30 years I had wanted to see the place for myself.

We anchored at the main island, Eilean Mor, with the lighthouse silhouetted above us through the clearing mist. Most of the steps in the side of the rock have been worn away by the sea, and all that remains of the handrail are a few rusting posts. We had to time our jump to the height of the 5 foot swell, and cling to the seaweed. We crawled up the side of the rock, 80 feet of scramble, to emerge on the top of the cliff. There a reception committee was waiting, clad in formal evening wear: several thousand tiny puffins stood and stared at us, curious, entirely without fear.

The lighthouse has been fully automated since the Seventies, when the last keepers departed, leaving the islands in perfect human isolation, save for the helicopter that lands once a year for the annual service by the Northern Lighthouse Board, and the odd rugged birdwatcher.

The sense of solitude was as penetrating as the mist. Here on the last outcrop of the Atlantic shelf, look in any direction and you see . . . nothing. Solitude brought St Flannan here in the first place. Below the lighthouse is the ruin of his "chapel", the tiny stone bothy where this resilient hermit reputedly spent several years in the 9th century. We crawled inside; the rising wind howled through the cracks between the stones. What must it have been like for the lighthouse keepers, cooped up in a brick tube for months, battered by wind, rain and waves? That was one of the many questions asked by Superintendent Robert Muirhead, who was dispatched by the Northern Lighthouse Board in January, 1901, to try to solve the Flannan Islands mystery.

Muirhead studied the weather, the tides, and the logs of every ship in the area. He interviewed the families of the vanished men, the people of Lewis and the ocean. A man of the modern age, an engineer, Muirhead was plunged into a world of ancient superstitions.

Some claimed that the men had been devoured by sea monsters, or spirited away by the angry spirit of Flannan. The poet Wilfred Wilson Gibson whipped up controversy by writing a ghostly poem imagining that the men had turned into three great black birds, and plunged into the sea. Newspapers luridly speculated that the men had fallen out, or been driven to madness and suicide by solitude, or the demon drink; it was rumoured that one man had murdered the other two, and then hurled himself from the cliff-top. The sailors and fishermen talked of the "Fist of God", the freak wave of ancient maritime legend, a rogue wall of water that rises suddenly out of the sea and pulls down ships and men, only to vanish again.

Several aspects of the incident did not (and do not) add up. The superintendent dismissed the notion that the three men had been blown off the island by a mighty gust of wind, pointing out that since the wind was westerly that night, this would have forced them up to the island and away from the cliffs. About 100 feet above sea-level, safety railings had been wrenched out of shape. Muirhead reckoned a boulder must have crashed down from the ledge above, but the sight of the ironwork—"displaced and twisted in a manner difficult to believe unless actually seen"—spooked even him. Why had one of the men left the lighthouse building in his shirtsleeves? If some catastrophe had befallen the men, who had had time to bolt the entrance gate to the lighthouse? Above all, if the men had drowned, the prevailing tides should have swept the bodies towards the Hebrides. Despite an intensive search, no body was found.

We stood on the crumbling steps leading down to the north landing. Here the wind was so strong that it was easy to imagine a man being swept to his death from here; but three? Was there some tragic collision between new technology and ancient beliefs? Or was there a rational explanation? Muirhead concluded "that an unexpectedly large roller had come up on the Island, and swept them away with resistless force".

He was probably right. Recent satellite research has shown that rogue waves of immense height are a more frequent occurrence than previously believed, scientific fact rather than maritime folklore.

Ben Macintyre in *The Times Magazine,* 21st January, 2006 (slightly adapted)

QUESTIONS

		Marks	Code
1.	Explain why "the Flannan Islands have a good claim to be the most deserted place in Britain" (lines 2–3). **Use your own words** as far as possible.	2	U
2.	What is surprising about the expression "delighted terror" (line 5)?	1	A
3.	Why is the word "preyed" (line 9) appropriate here?	2	A
4.	Look at lines 15–21, and explain **in your own words** what the "mystery" was.	2	U
5.	Look at lines 24–27. Explain why any **one** example of the writer's **word choice** effectively makes it clear that the climb up to the lighthouse was a difficult one.	2	E
6.	Look at the words "formal evening wear" (line 28). Explain why this expression may seem **either** surprising **or** appropriate here.	2	A
7.	Choose an expression from lines 30–33, and show how it helps us to understand the meaning of "rugged" as it is used here.	2	U
8.	The writer tells us: "The sense of solitude was as penetrating as the mist" (line 34).		
	(i) What does the writer mean by a "sense of solitude"?	1	U
	(ii) Why is this an effective comparison or simile?	2	E
9.	Why does the writer use inverted commas round "chapel" (line 36)?	1	A
10.	Show how **one** example of the writer's **word choice** in lines 38–40 effectively conveys the hardships of the lighthouse keepers' lives.	2	E
11.	What do lines 43–44 tell us about the way Muirhead approached his task?	1	U
12.	Look at the sentence "A man of the modern age, an engineer, Muirhead was plunged into a world of ancient superstitions" (lines 45–46). How does one feature of the **imagery** help to suggest something about Muirhead's task?	2	A
13.	Write down an expression from the next paragraph which continues the idea introduced by "superstitions" (line 46).	1	U
14.	Show how the meaning of "luridly speculated" (line 50) is made clear in the rest of the paragraph.	2	A
15.	Look at lines 57–68. Identify **two** of the "aspects" of the events which "do not . . . add up". **Use your own words** as far as possible.	2	U
16.	Identify one feature of **sentence structure** in lines 69–72 which is appropriate for this story of mystery.	1	A
17.	Explain why any feature of the final paragraph (lines 75–77) helps to make these sentences a satisfying conclusion to the passage.	2	E
	Total	**(30)**	

[END OF QUESTION PAPER]

X115/102

NATIONAL QUALIFICATIONS 2008

THURSDAY, 15 MAY
2.05 PM – 2.50 PM

ENGLISH
INTERMEDIATE 1
Critical Essay

Answer **one** question only.

Each question is worth 25 marks.

Answer ONE question only, taken from any of the Sections A to E.

In all Sections you may use Scottish texts.

Write the number of the question in the margin of your answer booklet.

The following will be assessed:

- **the relevance of your essay to the question you have chosen**
- **your understanding of the main points of the text(s) through some reference to the relevant areas of content**
- **your explanation of the ways in which aspects of structure/style/language contribute to the meaning/effect/impact of the chosen text(s)**
- **your personal reaction to the content or style of the text(s) supported by some textual reference**
- **the quality and technical accuracy of your writing.**

Each question is worth 25 marks.

SECTION A—DRAMA

Answers to questions in this section should refer to such relevant features as: conflict, character, key scene(s), theme, plot . . .

1. Choose a play in which there is an important relationship between two of the characters.

Identify the relationship and go on to show how it develops and why, in your opinion, it is important in the play as a whole.

2. Choose a play which deals with an unpleasant aspect of life.

Show how the unpleasant aspect of life affects one or more of the characters in the play and say whether you sympathise with the character(s) or not.

SECTION B—PROSE

Answers to questions in this section should refer to such relevant features as: content, character, theme, imagery . . .

3. Choose a novel **or** short story which has an important turning point.

Say how the turning point was reached and go on to show how it affects the characters and the ending of the story.

4. Choose a novel **or** a short story **or** a piece of non-fiction which deals with a topic **or** a character **or** a place which interests you.

Describe the topic **or** the character **or** the place and show how the writer makes it interesting for you.

SECTION C—POETRY

Answers to questions in this section should refer to such relevant features as: content, word choice, theme, imagery, sound . . .

5. Choose a poem about a person who has to face difficulties or problems.

Say what the poem is about and show how the writer uses particular words and phrases to help you to sympathise with the person.

6. Choose a poem which creates an exciting **or** dramatic **or** sad atmosphere.

Say what the poem is about and go on to show what particular words or phrases help to create the atmosphere.

SECTION D—FILM AND TV DRAMA

Answers to questions in this section should refer to such relevant features as: character, use of camera, key sequence(s), editing, sound/music, plot, setting . . .

7. Choose a film with an opening sequence which captures your interest.

Say what interests you in the sequence and show how the sequence made a good beginning to the film as a whole.

8. Choose a film **or** TV drama* which deals with at least one important relationship.

Describe the relationship and show how the film or programme makers use the techniques of film or TV drama to keep you interested in the relationship.

*"TV drama" includes a single play, a series or a serial.

SECTION E—LANGUAGE

Answers to questions in this section should refer to such relevant features as: vocabulary, accent, dialect, tone, abbreviation, register . . .

9. Consider the language used in TV programmes targeted at young people.

Identify some ways in which the language is different from the language used in other television programmes. Why do you think this language is attractive to young people?

10. Consider the language used in advertisements related to some aspect of daily life such as food or drink or leisure pursuits or holidays.

By referring to specific examples say why you think some aspects of the language used are successful in persuading you to buy the product.

[*END OF QUESTION PAPER*]

[BLANK PAGE]

INTERMEDIATE 1

2009

[BLANK PAGE]

X115/101

NATIONAL QUALIFICATIONS 2009

FRIDAY, 15 MAY
1.00 PM – 2.00 PM

ENGLISH
INTERMEDIATE 1
Close Reading

Answer all questions.

30 marks are allocated to this paper.

Read the passage carefully and then answer **all** the questions, **using your own words where asked to do so**.

The questions will ask you to show that:

you understand **what** the writer has said (main ideas and supporting details) (**Understanding–U**);

you can identify **how** the writer has said it (techniques of structure and style) (**Analysis–A**);

you can comment on **how well** the writer has achieved his purpose (using appropriate evidence) (**Evaluation–E**).

A code letter (U, A, E) is used alongside each question to identify its purpose for you.

In this passage, the writer, John Simpson, looks back with surprising affection on an occasion when he was cheated.

ROBBED IN PRAGUE

I have only once in my life been robbed by experts.

It happened in Prague, the capital of the old Czechoslovakia, a few days after what everyone now calls the Velvet Revolution of 1989, when the Communist government was overthrown without a drop of blood being shed. Six years earlier, in 1983, I had made a film there about the way the secret police treated political and religious dissidents, those people who disagreed openly with the government. After that, not surprisingly, I was banned from the country.

When I flew in this time, without a proper visa, I gambled on the fact that the revolution was just starting, and I hoped the government officials I encountered would realise that things were about to change. At Prague airport the man behind the immigration desk looked at me and my passport very long and carefully. Then he examined a message which had come up on his computer. Presumably it told him I was "an enemy of the state". In the end he made up his mind to ignore it. He stamped my passport, and gave me a little wintry smile. I was back.

The next few days were wonderful. I had a ringside seat, from which I could watch the end of the whole unpleasant, rotten police state which the Russians had created in Czechoslovakia. Still, it took some time to introduce a new system, and many of the old laws still applied. For instance, changing foreign money into the local currency, called crowns, still had to be done in the long-winded, expensive way of the past. I was short of time, and so I decided to change my money with a tout on the street. That was still illegal, but I decided to take the risk.

I wandered down into the Old Town. Today this is the part that stays open until past midnight, but in those days the streets were quiet by seven-thirty. Most of the shops had closed. It was getting late to find anyone to change money. I walked up and down in my expensive coat, looking exactly like what I was—a Westerner looking for a deal.

It worked. A man came out of an old house and walked beside me. He spoke quietly and looked straight ahead. "You want to change money?" he said in good English.

I said I did.

"How much?"

Two hundred dollars, I told him. That was a lot of money in Prague.

"I'm working on the house here," the man whispered. "Come into the hall. It's safer."

I stepped into the hall. It was dark, but the light from the room with the workmen in it was enough for us to see to change money.

"So, two hundred dollars, that's 140,000 crowns," the man said.

I showed him my two bills of a hundred dollars each. He looked at them carefully, then handed them back to me and began counting out the Czech notes.

At that instant there was an explosion of rage, and a stocky man came charging down the stairs.

"Oh, no!" shouted the man who was counting out the money. "It's my foreman! He's a real Communist. Quick, give me the dollars. Here's your cash."

He shoved a thick wad of notes into my hand. "Run for it! He'll call the cops!"

I ran for it. What if the authorities caught me? Even now, when Communism was collapsing, I could be in trouble. It would be embarrassing for me, and for the BBC.

And yet, even while I was running, something was working away inside my head. How come, if it was so dangerous to be doing a deal with a Westerner, the man had shouted out a warning to me in English? That, surely, would be proof to the foreman that he was up to no good.

I slowed down. No policemen were running through the streets in search of me. I stopped in an alley and pulled the wad of money out of my pocket. There were a couple of one-hundred-crown notes on the top. But the rest seemed less familiar. I had a hollow feeling in my stomach as I looked at them. These notes were all Polish. There was huge inflation in Poland at that time, and the whole thick wad of money I held in my hand was worth about five dollars. If, that is, you could find anyone who would accept them.

I had been well and truly robbed.

I turned round and ran back. In the old house the workmen were just packing up, and I spoke to one of them. Yes, there had been a couple of men hanging around. They were probably up to no good, he said. One of the men had gone upstairs, though neither of them was supposed to be there. They weren't working on the house, or anything like that. They just came in off the street. He'd heard one of the men shouting. Had they stolen something from me?

"No, not at all," I said, "nothing like that. No, I'd just been asking the way."

"Oh, asking the way," said the workman with a little grin. "I hope he told you. So why did you come back?"

I didn't say anything and walked off. At first I was angry. Two hundred dollars was quite a lot of money to have lost. I felt such an idiot.

As I walked, the spires of the old city shone in the damp evening air. Everything seemed so beautiful. Now this country that I loved so much was free, and I had had the privilege of watching it happen. That was worth vastly more than two hundred dollars.

Adapted from John Simpson, *Twenty Tales from the War Zone*

QUESTIONS

		Marks	Cod
1.	(*a*) Explain **in your own words** why "the *Velvet* Revolution of 1989" (line 3) was unusual.	1	U
	(*b*) Why does the writer include the expression "those people who disagreed openly with the government" in lines 5–6?	2	A
2.	The writer says he "gambled" (line 8) when he flew into Prague "this time".		
	Explain **in your own words**		
	(*a*) why he thought he might **not** get into the country on this occasion;	1	U
	(*b*) why he thought he might get in.	1	U
3.	Explain the humour of the sentence "Presumably it told him I was 'an enemy of the state'" (lines 12–13).		
	Your answer may focus on **content** or **tone**.	1	A
4.	Explain what is surprising about the expression "wintry smile" (line 14).	2	A
5.	Comment on the effectiveness of the **metaphor** or **image** "a ringside seat" (line 15).	2	E
6.	The writer knew that changing money unofficially was "illegal" (line 21).		
	Write down the expression from earlier in the paragraph which introduces the idea of this activity being against the law.	1	U
7.	Look at lines 22–25, and then explain in your own words what problem the writer came up against when he tried to change his money.	1	U
8.	Explain how one example of the writer's **word choice** in lines 26–36 shows that the Czech man changing the money wanted to be cautious.	2	A
9.	Lines 37–41 convey a different mood from the quiet caution shown in lines 26–36.		
	(*a*) Show how an example of the writer's **word choice** effectively conveys this new mood.	2	E
	(*b*) How does the **punctuation** of the words spoken by the Czech man contribute to this mood?	1	A
	(*c*) How does any feature of the **sentence structure** of the words spoken by the Czech man match this mood?	1	A
10.	The writer tells us "something was working away inside my head" (line 44).		
	Using your own words as far as possible, explain fully what was worrying him.	3	U
11.	(*a*) According to lines 49–55, how had the man swindled the writer?	3	U
	(*b*) How did the writer feel when he realised he had been swindled, and how does he emphasise this?	2	A
12.	The workman asks the writer if he has had something stolen from him (line 61).		
	What does the workman think of the writer's answer, and how can we tell?	2	U/A
13.	From line 67 to the end of the passage, the writer reflects on this experience with pleasure.		
	Why is this feeling quite understandable or appropriate?	2	A
	Total	**(30)**	

[*END OF QUESTION PAPER*]

[BLANK PAGE]

[BLANK PAGE]

X115/102

NATIONAL QUALIFICATIONS 2009

FRIDAY, 15 MAY
2.20 PM – 3.05 PM

ENGLISH
INTERMEDIATE 1
Critical Essay

Answer **one** question only.

Each question is worth 25 marks.

Answer ONE question only, taken from any of the Sections A to E.

In all Sections you may use Scottish texts.

Write the number of the question in the margin of your answer booklet.

The following will be assessed:

- **the relevance of your essay to the question you have chosen**
- **your understanding of the main points of the text(s) through some reference to the relevant areas of content**
- **your explanation of the ways in which aspects of structure/style/language contribute to the meaning/effect/impact of the chosen text(s)**
- **your personal reaction to the content or style of the text(s) supported by some textual reference**
- **the quality and technical accuracy of your writing.**

Each question is worth 25 marks.

SECTION A—DRAMA

Answers to questions in this section should refer to such relevant features as: conflict, character, key scene(s), theme, plot . . .

1. Choose a play which involves conflict between relatives or friends or groups of people.

Show how the conflict arises and say whether you find the outcome of the conflict satisfactory or not.

2. Choose a play in which a character gains your sympathy because of the way he or she is treated by other characters.

Describe how the character is treated by the others, and how he or she reacts, and explain why you feel sympathy for the character.

SECTION B—PROSE

Answers to questions in this section should refer to such relevant features as: content, key incident, character, theme, imagery . . .

3. Choose a novel **or** short story which has an important relationship between two people, or between a person and a place.

Say why the relationship is important and explain what happens to it by the end of the story. Go on to say what you feel about the ending.

4. Choose a novel **or** a short story **or** a piece of non-fiction which deals with a subject which interests you or shocks you.

Say what the subject is and why it arouses these feelings in you.

SECTION C—POETRY

Answers to questions in this section should refer to such relevant features as: content, word choice, theme, imagery, sound . . .

5. Choose a poem which is mainly about one person's experience.

Describe the experience and show how the poet uses particular words and phrases to help to make it clear to you how the person feels about the experience.

6. Choose a poem which describes a place or an event.

Briefly identify the place or event and go on to show how the poet's use of particular words and phrases gives a very clear description of the place or event.

SECTION D—FILM AND TV DRAMA

Answers to questions in this section should refer to such relevant features as: character, use of camera, key sequence(s), editing, sound/music, plot, setting . . .

7. Choose a film **or** TV drama* which uses many special effects.

Describe some of the special effects and say what they add to your enjoyment of the film or TV drama* as a whole.

8. Choose an important character from a film **or** TV drama* who is involved in a conflict.

Describe the part he or she plays in the conflict and explain how the conflict is made memorable.

* "TV drama" includes a single play, a series or a serial.

SECTION E—LANGUAGE

Answers to questions in this section should refer to such relevant features as: vocabulary, accent, dialect, tone, abbreviation, register . . .

9. Consider the language used by groups of people who are all interested in the same sport, or hobby, or job, or who all live in the same place.

What words and phrases do they use which are special to them, and how do these words and phrases help the members of the group to get along with each other better?

10. Consider the language used in any two advertisements you are familiar with.

Say which advertisement is more successful in persuading you to buy the product and, by referring to particular examples, explain why you think one is better than the other.

[*END OF QUESTION PAPER*]

[BLANK PAGE]

INTERMEDIATE 1

2010

[BLANK PAGE]

X115/101

NATIONAL QUALIFICATIONS 2010

THURSDAY, 13 MAY
9.00 AM – 10.00 AM

ENGLISH
INTERMEDIATE 1
Close Reading

Answer all questions.

30 marks are allocated to this paper.

Read the passage carefully and then answer **all** the questions, **using your own words where asked to do so**.

The questions will ask you to show that:

> you understand **what** the writer has said (main ideas and supporting details) (**Understanding—U**);
>
> you can identify **how** the writer has said it (techniques of structure and style) (**Analysis—A**);
>
> you can comment on **how well** the writer has achieved his purpose (using appropriate evidence) (**Evaluation—E**).

A code letter (U, A, E) is used alongside each question to identify its purpose for you.

In this extract from his autobiography, the writer, Bill Bryson, remembers and reflects upon the time he was first taken to Disneyland by his parents.

MONEY WELL SPENT

My father returned home in unusually high spirits, and revealed his startling plans to take us away on a trip over Christmas to some mysterious place.

"You wait. You'll like it. You'll see," was all he would say, to whoever asked. The whole idea of it was unspeakably exciting—we weren't the type of people to do something so rash, so sudden, so unseasonal—but unnerving too, for exactly the same reasons. So on the afternoon of 16 December, when Greenwood, my elementary school, dispatched its happy hordes into the snowy streets to begin three glorious weeks of yuletide relaxation (and school holidays in those days, let me say, were of a proper and generous duration), the family Rambler was waiting out front, steaming extravagantly, even keenly, and ready to cut a trail across the snowy prairies. We headed west as usual, crossed the mighty Missouri River and made our way past Omaha. Then we just kept on going. We drove for what seemed like (in fact was) days across the endless, stubbly snow-blown plains. We passed one enticing diversion after another—Pony Express stations, buffalo licks, a pretty big rock—without so much as a sideways glance from my father. My mother began to look faintly worried.

On the third morning, we caught our first sight of the Rockies—the first time in my life I had seen something on the horizon other than a horizon. And still we kept going, up and through the ragged mountains and out the other side. We emerged in California, into warmth and sunshine, and spent a week experiencing its wonders—its mighty groves of redwoods, the lush Imperial Valley, Big Sur, Los Angeles—and the delicious, odd feel of warm sunlight on your face and bare arms in December: a winter without winter.

I had seldom—what am I saying? I had never—seen my father so generous and care-free. At a lunch counter in San Luis Obispo he invited me—*urged* me—to have a large hot fudge sundae, and when I said, "Dad, are you sure?" he said, "Go on, you only live once"—a sentiment that had never passed his teeth before, certainly not in a commercial setting.

We spent Christmas Day walking on a beach in Santa Monica, and the next day we got in the car and drove south on a snaking freeway through the hazy, warm, endless nowhereness of Los Angeles. At length we parked in an enormous parking lot that was almost comically empty—we were one of half a dozen cars, all from out of state—and strode a few paces to a grand entrance, where we stood with hands in pockets looking up at a fabulous display of wrought iron.

"Well, Billy, do you know where this is?" my father asked, unnecessarily. There wasn't a child in the world that didn't know these fabled gates.

"It's Disneyland," I said.

"It certainly is," he agreed, and he stared appreciatively at the gates as if they were something he had privately commissioned.

For a minute I wondered if this was all we had come for—to admire the gates—and if in a moment we would get back in the car and drive on to somewhere else. But instead he told us to wait where we were, and strode purposefully to a ticket booth where he conducted a brief but remarkably cheerful transaction. It was the only time in my life that I saw two $20 bills leave my father's wallet simultaneously. As he waited at the window, he gave us a broad smile and a little wave.

"Am I ill or something?" I asked my mother.

"No, honey," she replied.

"Is Dad ill?"

"No, honey, everybody's fine. Your father's just got the Christmas spirit."

At no point in all my life before or since have I been more astounded, more gratified, more happy than I was for the whole of that day. We had the park practically to ourselves. We did it all—spun gaily in people-sized teacups, climbed aboard flying Dumbos, marvelled at the exciting conveniences in the Monsanto All-Plastic House of the Future in Tomorrowland, enjoyed a submarine ride and riverboat safari, took a rocket to the moon. (The seats actually trembled. "Whoa!" we all said in delighted alarm.) Disneyland in those days was a considerably less slick and manicured wonder than it would later become, but it was still the finest thing I had ever seen—possibly the finest thing that existed in America at the time. My father was positively enchanted with the place, with its tidiness and wholesomeness and imaginative picture-set charm, and kept asking why all the world couldn't be like this. "But cheaper, of course," he added, comfortingly returning to character and steering us deftly past a souvenir stand.

The next morning we got in the car and began the thousand-mile trip across desert, mountain and prairie to Des Moines. It was a long drive, but everyone was very happy. At Omaha, we didn't stop—didn't even slow down—but just kept on going. And if there is a better way to conclude a vacation by not stopping in Omaha, then I don't know it.

From Bill Bryson, *The Life and Times of the Thunderbolt Kid* (slightly adapted)

QUESTIONS

		Marks	Code
1.	In the opening paragraph, we read that the writer's father returned "in unusually high spirits". Explain **in your own words** what this tells us about the father's character.	2	U
2.	Look at lines 3–6.		
	(*a*) The writer tells us that the trip was "unspeakably exciting" (line 4). **In your own words**, give **two** reasons why the family found the prospect of the trip "exciting".	2	U
	(*b*) As well as exciting, how else did the family find the prospect of the trip? Answer **in your own words**.	1	U
3.	Look at lines 7–9. Explain how any **one** example of the writer's **word choice** in these lines helps emphasise the fact that the writer has pleasant memories of Christmas time when he was a boy.	2	A
4.	Look at lines 9–10, where the author mentions the family Rambler (a make of car). What is surprising about the way he refers to it?	1	A
5.	What does "endless, stubbly, snow-blown" (lines 12–13) suggest about the plains?	1	A

QUESTIONS (continued)

Marks Code

6. Look at the sentence in lines 13–15.

(*a*) What is the function of the words in parenthesis (dashes)? **2 A**

(*b*) What does the fact that he did not give "so much as a sideways glance" suggest about the writer's father? **1 U**

7. The writer tells us that when he saw the Rocky Mountains, this was the first time he "had seen something on the horizon other than a horizon" (line 17).

What does this hint about the appearance of the countryside where he lives? **1 U**

8. Look at the expression "a winter without winter" (lines 21–22).

(*a*) What is surprising about this expression? **1 A**

(*b*) Show how **other words** in the context make clear what the writer means by "a winter without winter". **2 U**

9. Show with clear reference to the paragraph in lines 23–27 how the writer puts emphasis on the idea that his father is mean with his money. **2 A**

10. Show how any **one** example of the writer's **word choice** in lines 30–35 effectively conveys the idea that Disneyland was an impressive place. **2 E**

11. Look at lines 40–44.

Explain why it is appropriate for the writer to use the expression "remarkably cheerful" when referring to the "transaction" his father conducts. **2 A**

12. Look at lines 51–54.

The writer tells us that his family "did it all".

How does the **sentence structure** in these lines help convey this idea? **2 A**

13. What is the effect of the inclusion of "actually" (line 54)? **1 A**

14. The writer says (line 55) that Disneyland was not as "slick and manicured" then as it was to become.

What does this expression suggest about Disneyland today? **2 U**

15. The writer says that his father steered the family "deftly past a souvenir stand" (line 60). Why does this suggest the writer's father was "returning to character"? **1 U**

16. Consider the passage as a whole. Explain why any **one** aspect of this extract helps to make it an effective piece of autobiographical writing. **2 E**

Total (30)

[*END OF QUESTION PAPER*]

X115/102

NATIONAL QUALIFICATIONS 2010

THURSDAY, 13 MAY
10·20 AM – 11·05 AM

ENGLISH
INTERMEDIATE 1
Critical Essay

Answer **one** question only.

Each question is worth 25 marks.

Answer ONE question only, taken from any of the Sections A to E.

In all Sections you may use Scottish texts.

Write the number of the question in the margin of your answer booklet.

The following will be assessed:

- **the relevance of your essay to the question you have chosen**
- **your understanding of the main points of the text(s) through some reference to the relevant areas of content**
- **your explanation of the ways in which aspects of structure/style/language contribute to the meaning/effect/impact of the chosen text(s)**
- **your personal reaction to the content or style of the text(s) supported by some textual reference**
- **the quality and technical accuracy of your writing.**

Each question is worth 25 marks.

SECTION A—DRAMA

Answers to questions in this section should refer to such relevant features as: conflict, character, key scene(s), theme, plot . . .

1. Choose a play in which there is a character who changes during the course of the action.

Say what the character is like at the beginning of the play, and then go on to explain how he or she changes during the play.

2. Choose a play in which there is a key scene which you found particularly dramatic.

Say what happens in the scene, and then explain why you think it is important.

SECTION B—PROSE

Answers to questions in this section should refer to such relevant features as: content, key incident, character, theme, imagery, setting . . .

3. Choose a novel **or** a short story which interests you right from the beginning.

Say what interests you, and explain how the writer keeps you interested in the rest of the story.

4. Choose a novel **or** a short story **or** a piece of non-fiction in which there is a person towards whom you feel a strong emotion such as sympathy **or** hatred **or** admiration.

Say how you feel about the person, and explain why you feel this way.

SECTION C—POETRY

Answers to questions in this section should refer to such relevant features as: content, word choice, theme, imagery, sound . . .

5. Choose a poem in which a person or a place is described clearly.

Say who or what is being described, and then go on to show how the poet's use of language makes the description so clear.

6. Choose a poem which has an important message for you.

Say what the message of the poem is, and then go on to show how the poet uses particular words and phrases to make the poem's message clear.

SECTION D—FILM AND TV DRAMA

Answers to questions in this section should refer to such relevant features as: character, use of camera, key sequence(s), editing, sound/music, plot, setting . . .

7. Choose a film **or** TV drama* which deals with a group of people within a community, workplace, neighbourhood, family . . .

Say who the key people in the group are, and explain how they maintain your interest in the film or TV drama.

8. Choose a scene or sequence from a film or TV drama* which has a sad **or** an exciting **or** a tense atmosphere.

Say what happens in the scene or sequence, and explain how the techniques of film or TV drama make this scene sad **or** exciting **or** tense.

* "TV drama" includes a single play, a series or a serial.

SECTION E—LANGUAGE

Answers to questions in this section should refer to such relevant features as: vocabulary, accent, dialect, tone, abbreviation, register . . .

9. Consider the language used by a group of people with a common interest in, for example, an organisation, a sport, a hobby . . .

Give examples of the special words and phrases used by the group and say why these words and phrases are interesting.

10. Consider the language of advertisements which aim to persuade you to buy something, to support a charity **or** to take better care of your health.

Consider the language used in your choice of advertisements and say why you think these advertisements are successful.

[*END OF QUESTION PAPER*]

[BLANK PAGE]

INTERMEDIATE 1

2011

[BLANK PAGE]

X270/101

NATIONAL QUALIFICATIONS 2011

FRIDAY, 13 MAY
1.00 PM – 2.00 PM

ENGLISH
INTERMEDIATE 1
Close Reading

Answer all questions.

30 marks are allocated to this paper.

Read the passage carefully and then answer **all** the questions, **using your own words where asked to do so**.

The questions will ask you to show that:

you understand **what** the writer has said (main ideas and supporting details) (**Understanding—U**);

you can identify **how** the writer has said it (techniques of structure and style) (**Analysis—A**);

you can comment on **how well** the writer has achieved his purpose (using appropriate evidence) (**Evaluation—E**).

A code letter (U, A, E) is used alongside each question to identify its purpose for you.

IN THE DRIVING SEAT

In this article Lucy McDonald looks into the world of women lorry drivers.

Think of long-distance lorry driving and the images that spring to mind are of burger stands in lay-bys, Yorkie bars and hairy male drivers. But next time you are on the motorway, take a second look at who is behind the wheel of that juggernaut in the slow lane. You may be surprised.

Once a rare sight on British roads, women lorry drivers are increasing in number. Better technology has made the driving easier and, along with female-friendly policies from companies, is helping to erode what was once the sole preserve of men.

According to industry experts, demand for qualified drivers currently outstrips supply and there is a deficit of up to 80,000. Although drivers say that the recession means there is less work, attracting more women to the job could solve a potential long-term recruitment problem. And more professional women are finding the prospect of life on the road appealing.

Kaz Horrocks is a long-distance lorry driver. "I was bored in my old job," she says, "and I enjoy the solitude of driving. Every day is different—sometimes I see amazing sunsets and lambs playing in the fields. I love it when you see the year's first hawthorn blossom and know that spring is near."

Neither hawthorn nor lambs are in evidence when I meet Kaz at six o'clock one dismal June morning in a lorry park. About 100 lorries have overnighted here. They are in lines, slumbering giants on the asphalt, their cab curtains drawn tightly as the drivers sleep inside.

As much as 99 per cent of Britain's freight is delivered by road, so next time you are stuck behind a lorry remember that without this workforce there would be no food on the table. This morning Kaz is taking me to deliver frozen meat. Inside her 40-tonne lorry, the cab is almost militarily neat with bunk beds, lots of ingenious storage and a kettle.

We sail around the M25 with a mighty view for miles ahead. "Chelsea tractors" have nothing on us—the windscreen is almost cinematic in its scope. Radio 2 is burbling in the background as we glide along. I am just a tourist, of course—for full-time female truckers the reality of work has its downsides, too. Until recently many truck stops had only male loos, and sleeping overnight in the cab alone would deter many women.

"I've never felt unsafe, though," says Kaz. "There is a certain amount of curiosity from the men about why I'm driving a truck instead of working at a desk but, apart from the occasional snide remark, most of the guys are really friendly."

The lifestyle is solitary by nature, but even more so for women. "There is a male camaraderie that I am excluded from," Kaz says. "It takes a particular kind of woman to drive a truck. It isn't something that a supermodel is going to do—you have to be a tough cookie."

Personally, I enjoy the open road. I feel free when I'm alone in the car, driving far away with nothing for company but my CD collection and talk radio. The journey appeals more than the destination: no bickering children or phone calls, nothing that must be dealt with. And how much more glorious that detachment would feel if you were 6 ft above other road users . . .

The only way to test this happy vision against the other realities that Kaz describes—traffic jams, tight deadlines, aggressive drivers and machismo—is to hit the road myself, although as someone who failed her driving test four times years ago I approach the challenge of HGV training with no little trepidation.

The HGV training normally takes five days, but my instructor has just a morning to show me the rudiments. I climb the ladder into a shiny 17-tonne lorry and feel a shiver as I turn on the ignition. The roar as its engine awakens sends vibrations through my whole body. The lorry is 27 ft (8·2 m) long and 12 ft 6 in (3·8 m) high. My little car would fit quite comfortably in its cabin—possibly twice over. It has 350 horsepower (I am not really sure what this means but it certainly sounds impressive). There are eight gears and no dual control, which does not seem to worry my instructor in the slightest, even when I reveal my chequered driving-test record.

I thrust the giant gearstick into first and ease my foot tentatively off the clutch. In principle it is just like in a car, but in practice the difficulty of everything required—effort, concentration, even aim—has been multiplied many times. I start moving and, for the first time in 20 years, remember why I never go on rollercoasters. The excitement is tremendous but so is the fear of something so powerful. I am not only in the grip of a monster but, supposedly, in control of it.

Within 30 minutes I am soaring around the training ground, doing nifty turns and even managing to reverse into a tight parking space. "Despite all the jokes, women are far better drivers than men," my instructor says. "That's why they are cheaper to insure. It's because they can multi-task. I know it's a cliché but it's true. They are better pupils, too—they don't think they know it all as soon as they sit behind the wheel."

The national pass rate for the HGV test is 34 per cent, and although there are no gender-specific statistics available he reckons that the pass rate for women is more like 70 per cent. Improved technology, in particular power steering, has made it easier for women to drive such large vehicles.

Yet the driving itself is only one battle in the war to win female hearts and minds—and the easiest. The industry has been male-dominated for so long that life on the road can still be difficult for women, even though equal opportunities legislation has helped.

Adapted from an article by Lucy McDonald in *The Times*

QUESTIONS

		Marks	*Code*
1.	Look at lines 1–7 and then explain **in your own words as far as possible** why we "may be surprised" nowadays when on a motorway.	**2**	**U**
2.	Look at lines 8–12, and then explain fully **in your own words** what the "recruitment problem" (line 11) is.	**2**	**U**
3.	Look at lines 13–16, and then explain why what Kaz says helps to make clear why she prefers lorry-driving to her old job.	**2**	**A**
4.	Explain why the sentence in lines 17–18 works well as a link between paragraphs.	**2**	**A**
5.	Look at the sentence in lines 21–23, and then explain how any feature of this sentence helps to get across the writer's argument. Your answer may concentrate on **content** or on any other feature such as **word choice**, **structure** or **tone**.	**2**	**A/E**
6.	Comment on the effectiveness of the expression "militarily neat" (line 24) as an **image** or **metaphor**.	**2**	**E**

QUESTIONS (continued)

Marks Code

7. Look at the lines 26–30.

(*a*) Explain the writer's use of inverted commas round the expression "Chelsea tractors" (line 26). **1 A**

(*b*) Explain the appropriateness of "burbling" in line 27. **1 A**

(*c*) Explain why the writer calls herself "just a tourist" (line 28). **1 U/A**

8. In line 31, Kaz Horrocks says that she has "never felt unsafe".

Explain **in your own words** why this is the case. **2 U**

9. We read in line 34 that "The lifestyle is solitary by nature, but even more so for women".

Explain **in your own words** why this is so. **2 U**

10. In line 38, the writer tells us that she feels "free" on the open road.

Write down the expression from later in the paragraph that sums up her feeling about the experience of driving. **1 U**

11. Why does the writer use dashes in lines 43–44? **1 A**

12. Look at lines 43–54, and then explain what the writer means when she refers to her "chequered driving-test record" (line 54). **2 U**

13. Look at lines 55–60.

Identify **one** example of **contrast** in the writer's word choice. **2 A**

14. Look at lines 61–62, and then show how **one** example of the writer's **word choice** illustrates a point about how her driving improved. **2 A**

15. The driving instructor claims that women "are better pupils" (lines 64–65).

What piece of evidence in the *next* paragraph goes some way towards proving his point? **1 A**

16. Think about the passage **as a whole**.

Explain with reference to the text which of these you think is the main purpose of this article:

(*a*) to entertain and inform;

(*b*) to argue or persuade. **2 E**

Total (30)

[*END OF QUESTION PAPER*]

X270/102

NATIONAL QUALIFICATIONS 2011

FRIDAY, 13 MAY
2·20 PM – 3·05 PM

ENGLISH
INTERMEDIATE 1
Critical Essay

Answer **one** question only.

Each question is worth 25 marks.

Answer ONE question only, taken from any of the Sections A to E.

In all Sections you may use Scottish texts.

Write the number of the question in the margin of your answer booklet.

The following will be assessed:

- **the relevance of your essay to the question you have chosen**
- **your understanding of the main points of the text(s) through some reference to the relevant areas of content**
- **your explanation of the ways in which aspects of structure/style/language contribute to the meaning/effect/impact of the chosen text(s)**
- **your personal reaction to the content or style of the text(s) supported by some textual reference**
- **the quality and technical accuracy of your writing.**

Each question is worth 25 marks.

SECTION A—DRAMA

Answers to questions in this section should refer to such relevant features as: conflict, character, key scene(s), theme, plot . . .

1. Choose a play in which there is conflict between two characters.

Say what caused the conflict and show how the writer develops it throughout the play.

2. Choose a play in which there is an important incident which acts as a turning point.

Describe the important incident and show how it affects the rest of the play.

SECTION B—PROSE

Answers to questions in this section should refer to such relevant features as: content, key incident, character, theme, imagery, setting . . .

3. Choose a novel **or** a short story which you enjoyed because of your interest in an important character.

Say how the writer makes the character interesting for you throughout the novel or short story.

4. Choose a novel **or** a short story **or** a piece of non-fiction which appealed to you because of its theme or topic.

Say what the theme or topic is and show how the writer makes it appealing.

SECTION C—POETRY

Answers to questions in this section should refer to such relevant features as: content, word choice, theme, imagery, sound . . .

5. Choose a poem which creates a particular feeling in the reader such as fear, sadness, anger, joy . . .

Say what the feeling is and go on to show how the poet creates this feeling.

6. Choose a poem which describes an important incident.

Say what the important incident is and show how the poet uses words and phrases to describe it effectively.

SECTION D—FILM AND TV DRAMA

Answers to questions in this section should refer to such relevant features as: character, use of camera, key sequence(s), editing, sound/music, plot, setting . . .

7. Choose a film **or** TV drama* in which a character has to face a problem.

Describe the problem, and explain how the film **or** programme makers show the character dealing with it.

8. Choose a film **or** TV drama* in which there is an exciting ending.

Describe briefly the exciting ending, and explain how the film **or** programme makers create the excitement.

* "TV drama" includes a single play, a series or a serial.

SECTION E—LANGUAGE

Answers to questions in this section should refer to such relevant features as: vocabulary, accent, dialect, tone, abbreviation, register . . .

9. Consider the language used by a particular group of people.

Give examples of the special words and phrases used by the group, and explain why they are useful and interesting.

10. Consider the language of any advertisement **or** group of advertisements that you have studied.

Give examples of the language used in your choice of advertisement(s) and say why you think these examples are effective.

[*END OF QUESTION PAPER*]

[BLANK PAGE]

INTERMEDIATE 1

2012

[BLANK PAGE]

X270/10/01

NATIONAL QUALIFICATIONS 2012

WEDNESDAY, 16 MAY
9.00 AM – 10.00 AM

ENGLISH
INTERMEDIATE 1
Close Reading

Answer all questions.

30 marks are allocated to this paper.

Read the passage carefully and then answer **all** the questions, **using your own words where asked to do so**.

The questions will ask you to show that:

you understand **what** the writer has said (main ideas and supporting details) (**Understanding—U**);

you can identify **how** the writer has said it (techniques of structure and style) (**Analysis—A**);

you can comment on **how well** the writer has achieved his/her purpose (using appropriate evidence) (**Evaluation—E**).

A code letter (U, A, E) is used alongside each question to identify its purpose for you.

SKIRL POWER

In this article, the writer tells us that the skirl, or sound, of the pipes is being heard again – and not only in Scotland.

Tucked away close to London Bridge, the Mudlark Pub might normally take a while to find. Tonight, however, you could locate it blindfold. Upstairs, as out of place as a troupe of Oxfordshire morris dancers round the back of Glasgow Central Station, five pipers are playing their hearts out. Even with the windows closed the decibel levels are substantial. They are Manawatu, a Scottish pipe band from New Zealand, whose unison playing is so precise that it sounds like a single instrument. Towards the end they march downstairs into the street where they do a moonlit lap of honour, watched by a slightly bemused-looking crowd.

The Great Highland Bagpipe is an instrument that inspires almost fanatical levels of passion, despite the fact that most players don't even make a living from it. But it is a passion I want to share. And I'm not alone. Piping is on the up. In Scotland, new pipe bands are springing up, and even in London a growing demand has meant that organised classes for adults have started, apparently for the first time since the 1930s. Run by the Scottish Piping Society of London, they cost around £10 for two hours – probably the best-value music tuition in the capital.

Some students have Scottish roots. Others, like me, simply like the idea of a challenge. A competent violinist and pianist and basic recorder player, I've even dabbled in the ukulele. 'So why not tackle the bagpipes?' I think, as I eye a YouTube performance by the Red Hot Chilli Pipers, the closest thing the piping world has to pin-ups. They have teamed the bagpipe with electric guitars and keyboard, punching out dazzling arrangements of rock anthems, attracting new audiences and players in the process.

Adam Sanderson, the vice-president of the society, is swift to reduce my ambitions to more modest levels. "We get lots of calls from men who say, 'I had a Scottish father and I want to learn the bagpipes in two weeks so I can play at my daughter's wedding,'" he says.

But nothing about the bagpipe is easy. The hand position is deceptively like the recorder yet, as Sanderson says, "halfway between and upside down", and the tuning is based on an ancient scale. Most woodwind instruments have a single or double reed. The bagpipe has four. Moisture can flatten the sound; warmth raise it. Simply achieving accurate tuning can be a minor miracle. Then there's the chanter.

With just nine basic notes, pipers use nifty fingerwork that gives the illusion of playing more notes than are actually possible. Modern technology makes life easier. Synthetic reeds keep their pitch for longer. Pipe bags now come with a Gore-Tex lining. And for the "wet" player there are moisture-control systems – boxes filled with absorbent cat litter.

To find out more about what's involved, I go to the Pipe Band World Championships in Glasgow, where judges take just a day to work their way through more than 200 bands from as far away as Australia and Pakistan. It can seem like an inward-facing event. Literally so. As the bands play the marches, reels and strathspeys known as Ceòl Beag, or light music, they turn away from the audience, watching each other so they don't drop a note.

"It gets under your skin," says Alan McGeachie, who plays the pipes and is a drummer with the Strathclyde Police Pipe Band, 12 times winners in the world championships. "It's in your blood. If you decide to leave, you think: 'Thank God I'm away from it', and suddenly it grabs you. It'll be with you to your last day."

Which is why, early one morning, I am in a rugby clubhouse in South London to get a preview lesson with Alasdair Smith, one of the instructors of the London piping classes. I've attempted to get to grips with the fingering, using a practice chanter to honking effect. Then I get to try out a full set of pipes – something that, in reality, no beginner would attempt for months. I blow into the bag like a breathalyser. Instead of there being constant pressure to force the air into the drones and chanter, seamlessly topping up the reservoir of air as I go, the bagpipe "sirens" horribly. Only by blocking two of the three drones do I get near a continuous note.

Then Smith plays a piece from the bagpipe's classical repertoire, developing into increasingly complex variations. Even to my ears, it's light years away from my enamel-stripping efforts. Piping can become an all-consuming obsession, he says. "I wouldn't want to sell it to anyone. It is enormously difficult and it's a long journey, a striving for perfection. When you're well tuned and well set up, it's uniquely captivating. That's what pipers are striving for." Unfortunately for my neighbours, I'm beginning to have an inkling of what he means.

Charlotte Phillips, in *The Times*

QUESTIONS

		Marks	*Code*
1.	The writer tells us that the Mudlark Pub "might normally take a while to find" (lines 1–2). Explain **as far as possible in your own words** why this is the case.	1	**U**
2.	Why is it appropriate for the writer to use "however" in line 2?	2	**A**
3.	How effective do you find the comparison "as out of place as a troupe of Oxfordshire morris dancers round the back of Glasgow Central Station" (lines 2–3)?	2	**E**
4.	Explain **in your own words** what is meant by "the decibel levels are substantial" (lines 4–5).	2	**U**
5.	Why does the writer find it surprising that "The Great Highland Bagpipe is an instrument that inspires almost fanatical levels of passion" (lines 9–10)? Explain as far as possible **in your own words**.	1	**U**
6.	Explain **in your own words two** pieces of evidence the writer gives to support her claim that "Piping is on the up" (line 11).	2	**U/A**
7.	**Using your own words as far as possible**, give **two** reasons why the writer thought she might "tackle the bagpipes" (line 18).	2	**U**

QUESTIONS

		Marks	*Code*
8.	What does the writer suggest about the group the Red Hot Chilli Pipers by comparing them to "pin-ups" (line 19)?	**1**	**U**
9.	Explain why any example of the writer's **word choice** in the sentence in lines 19–21 effectively conveys how impressive the band are.	**2**	**A**
10.	The writer says "reduce my ambitions to more modest levels" (lines 22–23). Explain **in your own words** what this means.	**2**	**U**
11.	Explain why the sentence "But nothing about the bagpipe is easy" (line 26) works well at this point in the passage.	**2**	**A**
12.	Explain why the writer uses inverted commas round "wet" (line 34).	**1**	**A**
13.	Why does the writer include the expression "or light music" (line 40)?	**1**	**U/A**
14	The player Alan McGeachie says that pipe music "gets under your skin" and is "in your blood" (lines 42–44). Explain how **one** expression later in the paragraph shows what he means.	**2**	**A**
15.	Look at lines 48–52. Explain how any expression from these lines shows that the writer is not impressed by the **sounds** she makes.	**2**	**A**
16.	Explain how effective you find any part of the expression "light years away from my enamel-stripping efforts" (lines 55–56) in illustrating the difference between Alasdair Smith's playing and the writer's.	**2**	**E**
17.	Explain why it is unfortunate for her neighbours that the writer is beginning to see what Smith means (see lines 59–60).	**1**	**U**
18.	Think about the passage as a whole. Why might "Skirl Power" be considered an appropriate title for this article?	**2**	**E**

Total (30)

[*END OF QUESTION PAPER*]

X270/10/02

NATIONAL QUALIFICATIONS 2012

WEDNESDAY, 16 MAY
10.20 AM – 11.05 AM

ENGLISH
INTERMEDIATE 1
Critical Essay

Answer **one** question only.

Each question is worth 25 marks.

Answer ONE question only, taken from any of the Sections A to E.

In all Sections you may use Scottish texts.

Write the number of the question in the margin of your answer booklet.

The following will be assessed:

- **the relevance of your essay to the question you have chosen**
- **your understanding of the main points of the text(s) through some reference to the relevant areas of content**
- **your explanation of the ways in which aspects of structure/style/language contribute to the meaning/effect/impact of the chosen text(s)**
- **your personal reaction to the content or style of the text(s) supported by some textual reference**
- **the quality and technical accuracy of your writing.**

Each question is worth 25 marks.

SECTION A—DRAMA

Answers to questions in this section should refer to such relevant features as: conflict, character, key scene(s), theme, plot . . .

1. Choose a play which has an important concern (such as teenage issues, poverty, family matters . . .).

Say what the concern is and go on to show how successfully **or** unsuccessfully it is dealt with by at least one of the characters.

2. Choose a play which has a scene which you would regard as important.

Say what happens in this scene and explain why you think it is important in the play as a whole.

SECTION B—PROSE

Answers to questions in this section should refer to such relevant features as: content, key incident, character, theme, imagery, setting, description, ideas . . .

3. Choose a novel **or** a short story **or** a piece of non-fiction **or** a group of texts which deals with a subject that you found amusing **or** sad **or** that made you angry.

Say what the subject is and why it aroused these feelings in you.

4. Choose a novel **or** a short story which has a frightening **or** a surprising incident.

Describe the incident and show how the author's description of the incident and the characters involved makes it frightening or surprising.

SECTION C—POETRY

Answers to questions in this section should refer to such relevant features as: content, word choice, theme, imagery, sound . . .

5. Choose a poem which describes an important incident **or** event.

Say what the important incident **or** event is and show how the poet uses words and phrases to describe it clearly.

6. Choose a poem which has an important message for you.

Say what the message of the poem is, and then go on to show how the poet makes the message clear.

SECTION D—FILM AND TV DRAMA

Answers to questions in this section should refer to such relevant features as: character, use of camera, key sequence(s), editing, sound/music, plot, setting . . .

7. Choose a film **or** TV drama* that is concerned with present-day problems.

Say what the problems are and show how they are presented in an interesting way.

8. Choose a key scene **or** sequence from a film **or** TV drama* which creates a turning point.

Describe what happens in the scene **or** sequence, and explain why this scene is important to the film **or** TV drama as a whole.

* "TV drama" includes a single play, a series or a serial.

SECTION E—LANGUAGE

Answers to questions in this section should refer to such relevant features as: vocabulary, accent, dialect, tone, abbreviation, register . . .

9. Consider the language of advertising aimed at a specific age group of people.

Explain some of the language features used and show how these features would appeal to your chosen age group.

10. Consider any aspect of language use which you have studied and enjoyed.

Explain which aspect of language use you most enjoyed studying in your investigation and go on to explain why you would encourage other people your age to carry out a similar investigation.

[*END OF QUESTION PAPER*]

Acknowledgements

Permission has been sought from all relevant copyright holders and Bright Red Publishing is grateful for the use of the following:
The article 'The Island of Lost Souls: Flannan Mysteries' by Ben Macintyre © The Times/NI Syndication (2008 Close Reading pages 2 & 3);
An extract adapted from 'Twenty Tales in the War Zone' by John Simpson, published by Pan MacMillan, London. Copyright © John Simpson 2007 (2009 Close Reading pages 2 & 3).
An extract from 'The Life and Times of the Thunderbolt Kid' by Bill Bryson. Published by Black Swan. Reprinted by permission of The Random House Ltd (2010 Close Reading pages 2 & 3);
An extract from the article 'In The Driving Seat' by Lucy McDonald taken from The Times © The Times/NI Syndication 11 June 2009 (2011 Close Reading pages 2 & 3);
The article 'Skirl Power' by Charlotte Phillips © The Times/NI Syndication 29 Aug 2008 (2012 Close Reading pages 2 & 3).

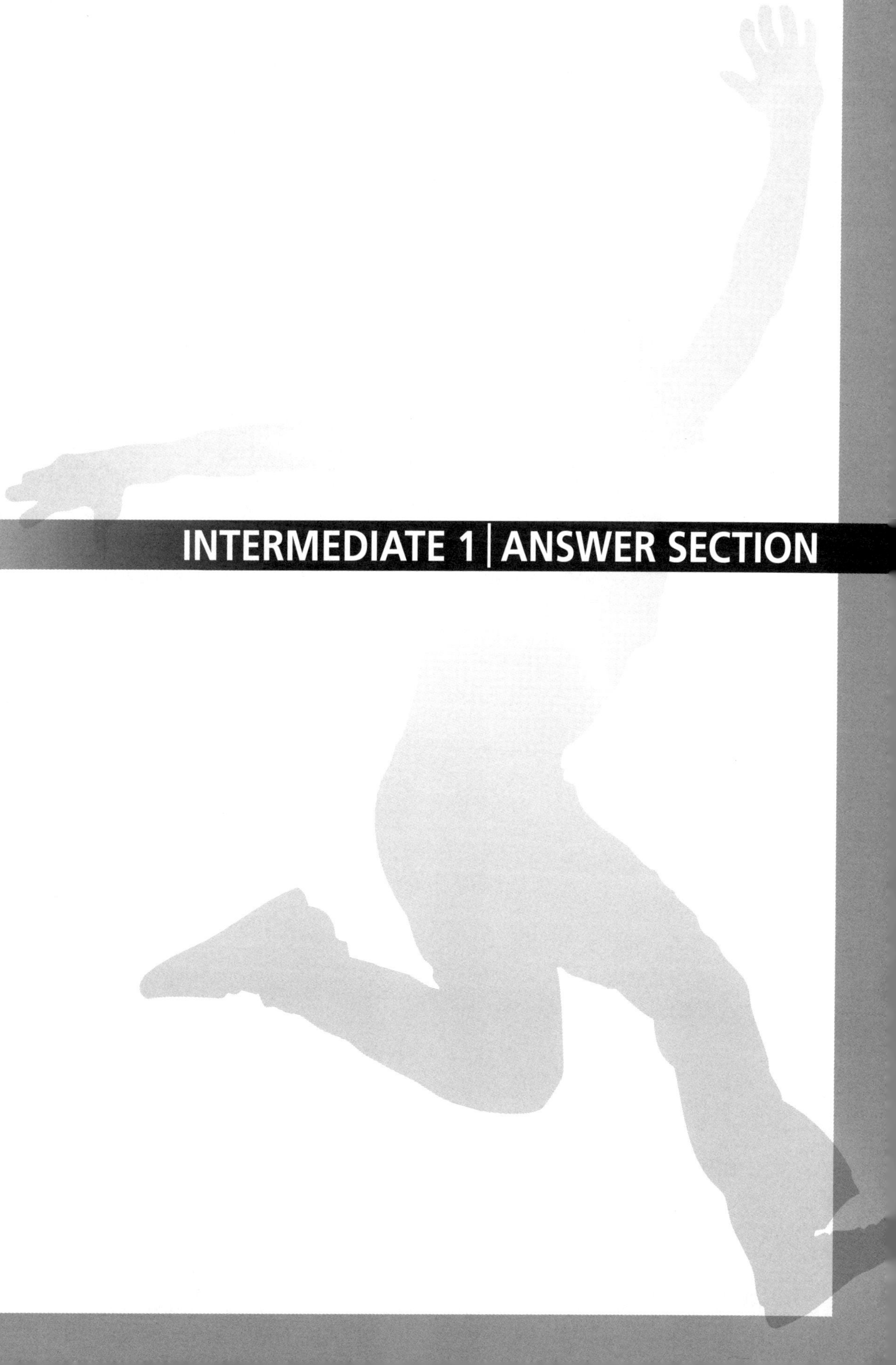

INTERMEDIATE 1 | ANSWER SECTION

BrightRED ANSWER SECTION FOR

SQA INTERMEDIATE 1 ENGLISH 2008–2012

ENGLISH INTERMEDIATE 1 CLOSE READING 2008

1. They are remote (gloss of "30 miles off the west coast of Lewis");
   They are barren (gloss of "lumps of rock");
   They are uninhabited (gloss of "The only inhabitants …")
   Any expanded comment on one of the above using your own words as far as possible.
2. The words contradict each other/are unusual with each other/are paradoxical/are an oxymoron.
3. It continues the idea/metaphor/image/ personification of "(Seven) Hunters"
   or
   the idea/metaphor/image/personification of "(Seven) Hunters" is connected with the losses of shipping
4. The lighthouse keepers had vanished
   Suddenly or for no obvious reason
   The men's lives had been disrupted (generalisation or paraphrase of example)
5. *Any one choice/comment from:*
   - Steps being "worn away"
     (clearly) showing the danger/perilousness of the ascent
   - "All that remains…are…posts"
     (clearly) shows there was nothing to hold on to
   - "(We had to time our jump to the height of) the 5 ft swell"
     (clearly) shows the (extent of the) danger/how testing it was
   - "cling"
     (clearly) shows how dangerous/taxing it was
   - "cling to the seaweed"
     (clearly) shows the lack of stable/firm handholds
   - "(We) crawled"
     (clearly) shows the slowness of progress
     or
     how it was impossible to stand upright
   - "80 ft"
     (clearly) shows the length/extent of the task
   - "scramble"
     (clearly) shows the climb to be strenuous/demanding
     or
     the shifting nature of the ground
6. *Surprising:*
   it (usually) refers to human clothes and here applies to the birds
   or
   it is associated with (elegant) special occasions and the setting is in the wilds
   Appropriate:
   it is black and white
   which is the birds' feather colouring
   or
   the areas of black and white look like a jacket and shirt
   or
   the expression reflects/repeats idea of or tone of "reception committee"
7. "The last keepers departed"
   or the island is "in perfect human isolation" **or**
   "the helicopter (that) lands once a year"
   And so any visitor would have to be hardy/self-sufficient/resilient/strong/robust/able to look after him or herself
8. (i) Feeling of loneliness/being alone/seclusion
   (ii) Just as the mist was unignorable/intrusive
   So the feeling (of loneliness) was strong/unsettling/inescapable
9. To show the vagueness or inappropriateness of the term/it's not really a chapel
10. *Any one choice/comment from:*
    - "Cooped up"
      (clearly) conveys the crampedness
    - "in a brick tube"
      (clearly) conveys the crampedness
      or
      the spartan nature of the accommodation
    - "for months"
      (clearly) conveys the long time they had to spend there
    - "battered"
      (clearly) conveys the harshness/severity of the weather
    - "wind, rain and waves"
      (clearly) conveys the multiplicity/variety of hostile elements
11. He was thorough/painstaking/professional/scientific
12. "(Muirhead was) plunged" suggests the suddenness/(figurative) depth/overwhelming nature of his task
    or his unpreparedness **or**
    the (implied) contrast with his usual life
    "world (of ancient superstitions)"
    suggests the size/complexity/range of the old beliefs he came across
    or
    the (implied) contrast with his usual life.
13. *Any one expression from:*
    - "(devoured by) sea monsters"
    - "spirited away"
    - "(the angry) spirit (of Flannan)"
    - "ghostly"
    - "turned into…birds"
14. There are a number of melodramatic/exaggerated/ sensational guesses/ideas/possibilities advanced
    or
    One example from madness/suicide/drink/murder/freak wave and comment on the fantastic/macabre/grotesque nature of that example
    or
    Quotation of "rumoured"
    and comment on the sensationalism/non-factual nature of eg murder/suicide
    There must be an understanding of luridness or speculation shown by quotation from/reference to elsewhere in the paragraph

15.

Originals	*References/paraphrases*
the wind was westerly that night	direction of the wind
The railings...had been wrenched out of shape **or** ironwork "displaced and twisted"	Severity/extent of the damage to the iron railings
One of the men left...in his shirtsleeves	One man left without putting on a coat
Bolt the entrance gate	The gate was locked
No body was found	No corpses were washed up (despite direction of tide)

16. (Frequent) use of (unanswered) questions.
Use of semi-colon

17. The facts (about big waves) solve the mystery
or
the mention of rogue waves recaps an idea previously mentioned (the "Fist of God")
or
"folklore" recaps the idea of superstition previously mentioned
or
the **alliteration** of "fact" and "folklore"
or
the **balance/contrast** of the two phrases "scientific fact" and "maritime folklore" is neat in its own right
or
"he was probably right" briefly/neatly sums up **or** provides a comforting tone
or
the contrast between short and long sentences is neat/elegant

ENGLISH INTERMEDIATE 1 CRITICAL ESSAY 2008

Please see Critical Essay Marking Principles on pages 63–64.

ENGLISH INTERMEDIATE 1 CLOSE READING 2009

1. (*a*) There was no violence/injury
   (*b*) It explains/clarifies/tells us what "dissidents" means

2. (*a*) He was proscribed/barred/prohibited/excluded (gloss of "banned")
   or
   Because he did not have the right/correct/required travel document/permission
   (*b*) There was an alteration of/development in the political circumstances/There was an expectation of leniency

3. Content – (obvious) exaggeration/hyperbole/ overstatement
Tone – (idea of being) laconic/self-deprecating/ ironic/sardonic **or** mock-seriousness of "enemy of the state"

4. "Wintry" suggests unfriendliness/cold whereas "smile" suggests friendliness/warmth

5. Derivation/sense of 'ringside seat' + relationship/appropriateness to writer's situation
Eg Just as a ringside seat is close to the action/affords a good view (at eg a circus or boxing match)
So he was very near to/witnessed clearly the (spectacular) end of Communism/the changes in the country.

6. '(a) tout (on the street)'

7. There were (very) few people around (gloss of "the streets were quiet").

8. Quotation of and comment on any of:

walked beside me	(eg) suggests concealment of ongoing transaction
He spoke quietly	(eg) does not wish to draw attention to himself
(he) looked straight ahead	(eg) does not wish to appear shifty/does not want to be seen talking to Simpson
the man whispered	(eg) does not wish to draw attention to himself
(Come into the hall.) It's safer.	(eg) shows concern about/awareness of danger
He looked at them carefully	(eg) shows wariness/prudence

9. (*a*) Any one of "explosion", "rage", "charging", "Oh, no!", "shouted", "Quick", "shoved", "Run for it" or "call the cops" (clearly) suggests tension/anxiety/ urgency **or** noise
   (*b*) Use of (several) exclamation marks
   (*c*) Very brief **or** (idea of) imperative **or** (cumulative effect of) list (of urgent instructions)

10. Some attempt at glosses of:

Although it was "dangerous to be doing a deal with a Westerner"	eg it was risky to do business with someone from the west
"the man had shouted out a warning ... in English"	eg the alarm had been called in English
Which was certain "proof ... that he was up to no good"	eg which is confirmation he was doing something wrong/illegal

11. (*a*) Underneath the Czech money on top
There was Polish money
Which was worth much less than/worth $2^1/_2$ % of his money
And/or very hard to change

(*b*) He felt empty/shocked
He uses "hollow feeling" **or** "well and truly";
or
He describes himself as having been "robbed";
or
He gives the sentence a paragraph to itself.
or gloss of "angry" (eg. cross) and reference to "At first I was angry" **or** foolish/embarrassed/and reference to "I felt such an idiot"

12. Incredulity/he does not believe him
Shown by any one of:
He grins/he says "I hope he told you"/the repetition of "asking the way"/he asks him why he came back/ appropriate comment on the tone he uses.

13. He had been swindled <u>by experts</u>
and he was happy to have paid for the experience/he has learned something
or
The (incipient) freedom of the country (which he loved) was (considerably) more valuable than his money

ENGLISH INTERMEDIATE 1 CRITICAL ESSAY 2009

Please see critical Essay Marking Principles on pages 63–64.

ENGLISH INTERMEDIATE 1 CLOSE READING 2010

1. Glosses of "unusually" and "high spirits"
eg he was normally less cheerful
Or he was more cheerful than usual

2. (*a*) *Any two from:*
Reference to "we weren't the type of people" – eg this was out of character
OR reference to "all he would say" – eg idea of mystery/suspense/lack of information
OR gloss of "rash" – eg impulsive/ill-advised/ impetuous/reckless
OR gloss of "sudden" – eg unexpected/happening at very short notice
OR gloss of "unseasonal" – eg at an unusual time of year

(*b*) Gloss of "unnerving" – eg frightening/scary/ unsettling/daunting/it made them nervous/uneasy

3. Quotation of and comment on any one of:

happy hordes	eg gives idea of enjoyment (for many) OR is alliterative
snowy streets	eg (stereotypical) attractive scene OR is alliterative
(three) glorious (weeks)	eg gives idea of intensity of pleasure
yuletide	eg suggests nostalgia (because it is old-fashioned)
relaxation	eg suggests (pleasurable) leisure, repose
school holidays (in those days) were … proper/generous	eg conveys sense of approval

4. Makes it sound as if it was human/was alive/had emotions; personifies it
OR reference to "steaming" + extrapolation – eg it is an unusual word to use to refer to a car/it is an internal combustion engine/or there is a lengthy journey imminent and it sounds as if it is malfunctioning

5. They go on for ever/were repetitive/boring/ unattractive/bleak

6. (*a*) They exemplify/illustrate what is meant by an "enticing diversion"
OR
They provide humour
By irony/the examples not being enticing

(*b*) He was determined to carry on OR he was not distracted by/interested in the things they passed/scenery

7. It is very flat/there are no hills/it is featureless

8. (*a*) It appears to contradict itself/idea of paradox

(*b*) "warm sunlight" or "bare arms"
suggests unseasonal weather/is unusual for December

9. *Any one expression plus comment – answer may be concerned with a feature of word choice, structure, typography or content*

Word choice

writes "what am I saying?"	which suggests/conveys inadequacy of "seldom"
uses "never"	which suggests lack of precedent
uses "urged"	which suggests shock at the unusual/unexpected generosity
"certainly not"	underlines the rarity of this

Structure

(Parallelism/ similarity of) "I had seldom … I had never"	draws attention to the contrast/rarity
repetition of "never"	confirms/underlines lack of precedent
use of parenthesis	draws attention to the writer's surprise (at his father's behaviour)
pairing of "seldom … never" or "invited … urged"	is use of/progression to a stronger word

Typography

italics on "urged"	suggest writer is surprised

Content

asks his father if he is sure	which suggests surprise
idea that this "sentiment … had never passed his teeth before"	confirms unprecedented nature of this invitation
Another example of the father's behaviour	+ explanation of how this highlights his meanness

10. *Any one example plus comment from:*

enormous parking lot	(clearly) suggests large-scale operation
a grand entrance	(clearly) suggests size/magnificence
fabulous display	(clearly) suggests it was remarkable/extraordinary
fabled gates	(clearly) suggests fame or near-magical quality

11. His father is in good spirits
Yet he is spending (an unprecedented sum of) money
The **unexpected** nature of his demeanour must be present for full marks.

12. List format
suggests multiplicity of activities
OR
Variety/number of verbs (accept "words") used
suggests diversity of activities
OR
Dash implies expansion
of "all"

13. To show the boy's wonder/to show the realistic effect (Then);
OR
to convey irony/idea of (retrospective) whimsy at the unspectacular device (Now)

14. It is (more) efficient/(better or) well-organised; accept also reference to the pejorative sense of insincerity/ superficiality (Result)
it is very neat/has been given a face-lift/make-over/has been done up (Process)

15. He was (adroit/skilful/smart/nifty/nimble at) avoiding spending money

16. The way the extract
- uses the first person narration/is written from the writer's point of view
- uses mainly sequential narrative
- reveals the writer's personality
- recreates characters/places that have influenced the writer
- provides details of the writer's history
- establishes setting in place/time
- recreates key experiences from the writer's life
- establishes rapport with the reader

plus comment on appropriateness to autobiographical writing

ENGLISH INTERMEDIATE 1 CRITICAL ESSAY 2010

Please see critical Essay Marking Principles on pages 63–64.

ENGLISH INTERMEDIATE 1 CLOSE READING 2011

1. an HGV / freight / wagon / truck driver
could well be female / a lady

2. shortfall in / insufficiency of / lack of (gloss of "demand outstrips supply" or "deficit")
experienced / trained / certified drivers (gloss of "qualified")

3. She likes being on her own OR the variety of (what she sees when she is) driving (lift or gloss of "solitude" or "Every day is different")
which is the opposite of the tedium / sameness / monotony of what she used to do (lift or gloss of "bored")

4. "hawthorn" or "lambs"
refers back to the previous paragraph

5. **Content**

Reference to 99% of freight being road-borne OR reference to (potential absence of) food	(effectively) shows how dominant / important road haulage is
Reference to being stuck behind a lorry	(effectively) shows writer's awareness that lorries can be irksome / acknowledges reality
Word choice	
(idea of) imperative "remember"	(effectively) is forceful / personal
or "workforce"	suggests (e.g.) unity of drivers
or reference to the alliteration	emphasises / draws attention to the expression
Structure	
Positioning of opening clause	(effectively) underlines the Importance of the statistic
or length of sentence	complements the idea of a long queue
Tone	
The forceful / severe / admonitory tone	(effectively) underlines the importance of lorry drivers
Register	
Use of second person "you" / direct addressing of the reader	(effectively) involves the reader / shows relevance of the argument to the reader
Typography	
Use of figures	(effectively / dramatically) clarifies argument

6. Just as army routine is well-ordered / disciplined / efficient so the cab is orderly / well-organised / tidy / systematic / efficiently laid out
or
The bunk beds
are redolent of a barrack-room

7. (*a*) To acknowledge slang term / (idea of) neologism / quotation of what other people call the vehicle / The car is not really a tractor

(*b*) Meaning: conveys sense of rambling / vacuity / continuity / lack of attention being paid to it / being at a low volume

Sound: (idea of) onomatopoeia / alliteration

(*c*) she is only visiting this lifestyle temporarily / for a limited period /
she is not full time (time)
superficially (depth)
She only sees the good things about the job
She is just a passenger, not the driver

8. (The majority of) her (male) colleagues are affable / nice / just interested
(gloss of "curiosity" or "(most of) the guys are really friendly")
or
There is only the odd mean / nasty / unpleasant / cutting / hurtful comment
(gloss of "the occasional snide remark")
or
She is resilient / hard (gloss of "tough cookie")
And therefore unlikely to be scared

9. She is barred from / prohibited from / not allowed in to / kept out of (gloss of excluded)
(masculine) bonding / comradeship / society / fellowship (gloss of cameraderie)

10. Detachment

11. The words are in parenthesis / they explain / exemplify (what the "realities" are) / indicate the addition of extra information

12. She was unsuccessful in her test
many times / more than once
Some attempt to gloss "someone who failed her driving test four times years ago"

13. (1) "thrust" and "ease" or "tentatively""
(2) "in principle" and "in practice"
(3) "excitement" and "fear"
(4)"in the grip" and "in control"

14.

Within 30 minutes	suggests speed of learning
soaring	suggests (e.g.) confidence
nifty	suggests (e.g.) adroitness
even	indicates particular difficulty of mastered manoeuvre
managing	suggests (new) accomplishment / ability
reverse into a tight parking space	indicates nature of mastered manoeuvre

15. Superior pass rate.

16. No marks for choice. Credit is given for a full answer which gives a valid substantiated point to support the choice, e.g.:

To entertain and inform
uses informal register to connect with reader + example
use of humour / stereotypes + example
use of dramatic description + example
provides many facts + example
quotes / uses appropriate figures / statistics + example
cites evidence from experts + example

To argue or persuade
obvious stance / commitment / conviction + example
use of supporting figures / statistics + example
use of expert witnesses + example
quotes direct testimony / opinions of lady driver + example
uses emotive language + example
forceful tone appropriate to argument + example

ENGLISH INTERMEDIATE 1 CRITICAL ESSAY 2011

Please see critical Essay Marking Principles on pages 63–64.

ENGLISH INTERMEDIATE 1 CLOSE READING 2012

1. Gloss of "tucked away" – eg hidden/not easily seen/inconspicuous/unobtrusive/discreet/out of the way
   or
   Idea of being overshadowed/dominated by London Bridge

2. There is a contrast between what is usual and what is happening on this occasion eg, "tonight is an exception"
   or
   Something different is happening on this occasion
   Lifts are acceptable, for example:
   "Because you could find it blindfold/easily on this occasion/tonight but/though it's usually hard to find"

3.

Effective	It suggests the unexpectedness/strangeness/incongruity/a difference of cultures of bagpipers and/or morris dancers in these settings E.g. "You wouldn't expect to see morris dancers in Glasgow **or** you wouldn't expect to see bagpipers in London"
Ineffective	The idea that the image doesn't work because of incomprehension of morris dancers is acceptable

4. Glosses of "decibel (levels)" and "substantial" – eg the noise/sound/music is loud
   or
   it is very loud

5. Gloss of "(most players) don't even make a living from it" – eg (most players) are amateur/do not make (much) money from their music

6. *Any two glosses of:*

"(In Scotland), new pipe bands are springing up"	eg fresh groups are being formed/ flourishing/starting
"(even in London) a growing demand"	eg more interest is being shown
"organised classes for adults have started (for the first time since the 1930s)"	eg learning groups have begun/tuition is available

7. *Any two glosses of:*

"(like the idea of a) challenge"	eg (she was up for / relished a) test/trial/ attempt/difficult thing
"competent (musician)"	eg she was reasonable/ capable/proficient/adept/ adequate
"violinist and pianist and basic recorder player"	eg she plays other instruments

   or
   She was inspired by the Red Hot Chilli Pipers

8. They are admired/good-looking/favoured by young people/famous

9.

teamed	suggests successful combination
punching (out)	suggests impact/rhythmic quality of the music
dazzling	suggests expertise of musicians/figurative pyrotechnic quality of music/effect on audience of music
attracting new audiences	suggests growing popularity of the music

10. to lower/make more realistic/make less grand her aspirations/hopes

11.

It provides a link to the idea of difficulty / between the ideas of ease and difficulty	ie linking function, explanation
or It is an effective topic sentence introducing the idea of lack of ease	ie introductory function, explanation

   or
   "But" introduces a contrast

12. To acknowledge the jargon/technical nature/vagueness/inaccuracy/euphemistic nature of the expression

13. To explain/clarify what is meant by (the Gaelic expression) "Ceòl Beag".

14. Quotation of either "it grabs you" or "It'll be with you to your last day" makes inescapable or fascinating or hereditary nature of activity clear

15.

honking (effect)	suggests resemblance to a harsh/intermittent sound **or** sound produced by a klaxon or goose (bird not instrument)
or sirens	suggests wavering/ululating/harsh/deterrent quality of sound
or "horribly"	suggests cacophony/unpleasantness

16.

light years away	(effectively) suggests the distance she is from competence
enamel-stripping efforts	(effectively) suggests the abrasive/discordant nature of her efforts (accept also reference to volume)

   Correct extrapolation without selective quotation may gain 1 mark.

17. *Any one idea from:*
   Her efforts will be loud/discordant/annoying
   or she will be playing for a long time

18. Identification of an aspect of the title relation to a feature of the passage eg

"skirl" refers to the pipes	and the passage is all about the pipes
"power" suggests potency	and the passage is all about their influence/their enduring appeal
"skirl power" is like/is a parody of "girl power"	and the writer is female

ENGLISH INTERMEDIATE 1 CRITICAL ESSAY 2008 TO 2012 EXAMS

Marking Principles for the Critical Essay are as follows:

- The essay should first be read to establish whether it achieves success in **all** the Performance Criteria for Grade C, including relevance and the standards for technical accuracy outlined in Note 1 below.
- If minimum standards are not achieved in any **one** or more of the Performance Criteria, the maximum mark which can be awarded is 11.
- If minimum standards have been achieved, then the supplementary marking grids will allow you to place the work on a scale of marks out of 25.
- The Category awarded and the mark should be placed at the end of the essay.

Notes:

1. *Mainly accurate*
Although a few errors may be present, spelling, vocabulary and sentence structures will be sufficiently accurate to convey the candidate's meaning at first reading

2. *Using the Category descriptions*
- Categories are not grades. Although derived from performance criteria at C and the indicators of excellence for Grade A, the four categories are designed primarily to assist with placing each candidate response at an appropriate point on a continuum of achievement. Assumptions about final grades or association of final grades with particular categories should not be allowed to influence objective assessment.

- Once an essay has been deemed to pass the basic criteria, it does not have to meet all the suggestions for Category II (for example) to fall into that Category. More typically there will be a spectrum of strengths and weaknesses which span categories.

GRADE C
Performance Criteria

(*a*) *Understanding*
As appropriate to task, the response demonstrates understanding of the main point(s) of the text(s) through some reference to relevant areas of content.

(*b*) *Analysis*
The response describes some of the more obvious ways in which aspects of structure/style/language contribute to meaning/effect/impact.

(*c*) *Evaluation*
The response contains a stated or implied personal reaction to the content or style of the text(s), supported by some textual reference.

(*d*) *Expression*
Language conveys meaning clearly and a generally relevant line of thought is discernible; spelling, grammar and punctuation are mainly accurate.

It should be noted that the term "text" encompasses printed, audio or film/video text(s) which may be literary (fiction or non-fiction) or may relate to aspects of media or language.

Language Questions 9 - 10

- The "text" which should be dealt with in a language question is the research which the pupil has done. Examples taken from their research must be there for you to see.
- However, to demonstrate understanding and analysis related to these examples there has to be some ability to make comparisons or to group words of similar kinds to make a point about the use of language.

Intermediate 1 Critical Essay Supplementary Advice

This advice, which is supplementary to the published Performance Criteria, is designed to assist with the placing of scripts within the full range of marks. However, the Performance Criteria as published give the primary definitions. The mark range for each Category is identified.

IV 8–11	III 12–15	II 16–19	I 20–25
An essay which falls into this category may do so for a variety of reasons. It could be • that it fails to achieve the criterion of "mainly accurate" • or that any knowledge and understanding of the material is not used to provide a discernible line of thought • or that personal reaction/opinion is unconvincing • or that discussion of techniques is not sufficiently related to the point being made • or that the answer is simply too thin.	<u>**Understanding**</u> • Knowledge of the text(s), and a **basic understanding** of the main point(s) will be used	<u>**Understanding**</u> • Knowledge of the text(s), and an **understanding** of the main point(s) will be used	<u>**Understanding**</u> • Knowledge of the text(s), and an **understanding** of the main point(s) or **central concerns** will be used
	to provide a **discernibly relevant** response to the question.	to provide a response **generally relevant** to the question.	to provide a response **relevant** to the question.
	• Some reference to the relevant **areas of content** will be made in the course of the response.	• Some reference to the **text(s) or more generally to its content** will be made in the course of the response.	• Some reference to the **text(s) as well as to its content** will be made in the course of the response.
	<u>**Analysis**</u> • There will be a **description** of some obvious techniques which add to the meaning or impact of the text(s).	<u>**Analysis**</u> • An **attempt** will be made **to explain** how some obvious techniques add to the meaning or impact of the text(s).	<u>**Analysis**</u> • There will be an **explanation** of how some obvious techniques add to the meaning or impact of the text(s).
	<u>**Evaluation**</u> • There will be some engagement with the text(s) and a **personal reaction** to it will be stated or implied.	<u>**Evaluation**</u> • There will be some engagement with the text(s) and a **personal opinion** will be stated or implied.	<u>**Evaluation**</u> • There will be some engagement with the text(s) and a **basic evaluation** will be stated or implied.
	<u>**Expression**</u> • Language will convey meaning clearly. Spelling, grammar and punctuation are mainly accurate.	<u>**Expression**</u> • Language will convey meaning clearly. Spelling, grammar and punctuation are mainly accurate.	<u>**Expression**</u> • Language will convey meaning clearly. Spelling, grammar and punctuation are mainly accurate.

BrightRED PUBLISHING

Published by Bright Red Publishing Ltd, 6 Stafford Street, Edinburgh, EH3 7AU
Tel: 0131 220 5804, Fax: 0131 220 6710, enquiries: sales@brightredpublishing.co.uk,
www.brightredpublishing.co.uk

Official SQA answers to 978-1-84948-262-2
2008-2012

OFFICIAL SQA PAST PAPERS WITH ANSWERS

INTERMEDIATE 1

ENGLISH
2008-2012

SQA

BrightRED PUBLISHING

First exam published in 2008.
Published by Bright Red Publishing Ltd, 6 Stafford Street, Edinburgh EH3 7AU
tel: 0131 220 5804 fax: 0131 220 6710 info@brightredpublishing.co.uk www.brightredpublishing.co.uk

ISBN 978-1-84948-262-2

A CIP Catalogue record for this book is available from the British Library.

Bright Red Publishing is grateful to the copyright holders, as credited on the final page of the Question Section, for permission to use their material. Every effort has been made to trace the copyright holders and to obtain their permission for the use of copyright material. Bright Red Publishing will be happy to receive information allowing us to rectify any error or omission in future editions.